KETO BREAD
COOKBOOK

Easy Keto Baking Recipes from Fragrant Bagels and Buns to Muffins and Breadsticks. Low-Carb and Gluten-Free Baking Recipes

Jennifer Tate

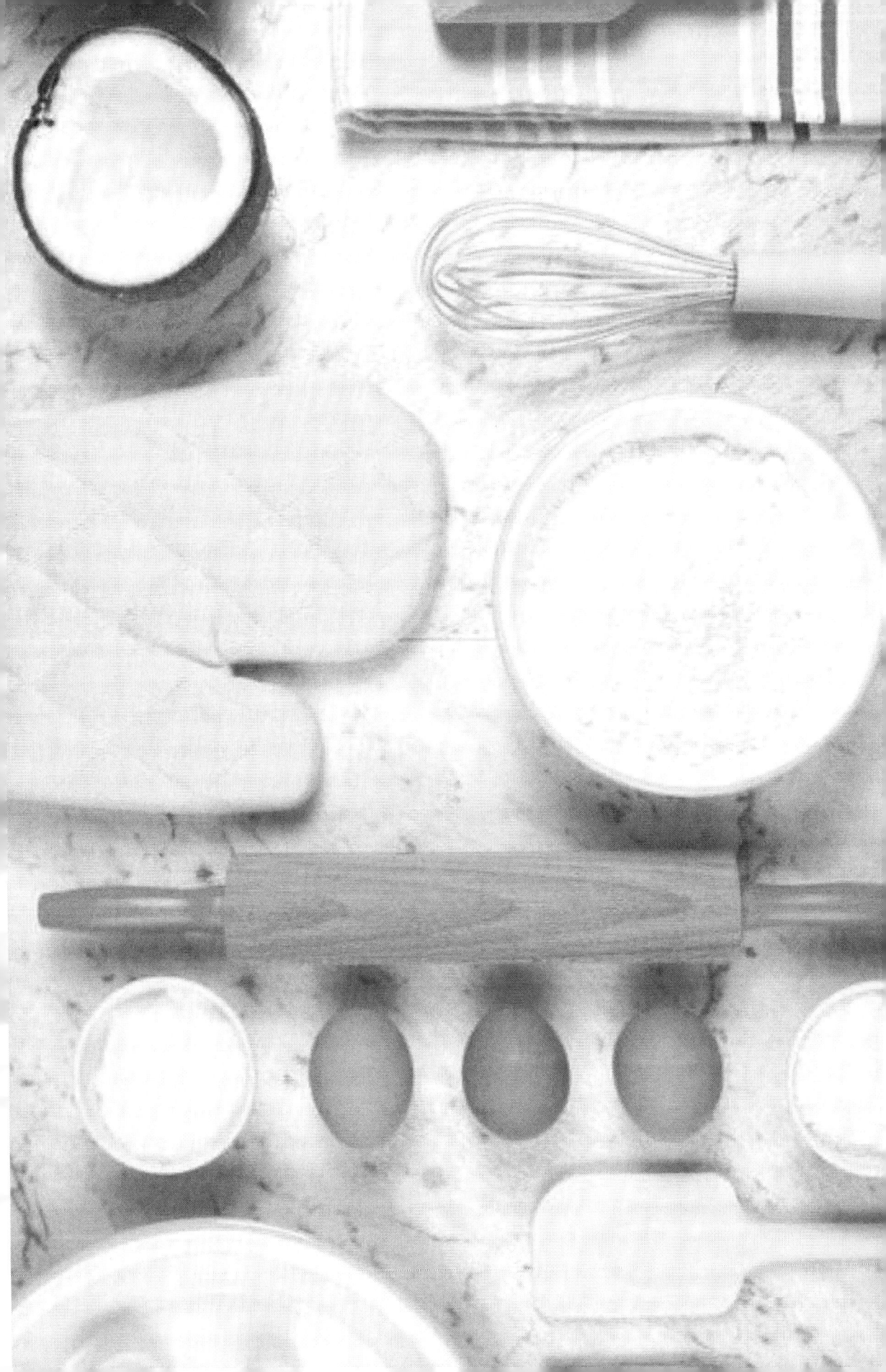

Contents

You CAN Eat Bread on a Keto Diet! 6

Basic Keto Bread 16

Energy Lunch Bread 30

Crispy Mediterranean Loaves 44

Nutritious Pizza and Tortillas 62

Assorted Buns & Bagels 74

Snack Breadsticks & Crackers 86

Delicate Muffins & Scones 100

Mouthwatering Waffles & Pancakes 114

Preface

Bread. We all love a tasty slice of bread from a **freshly baked loaf**. It's even better if that bread just came right out of the home oven!

But you've recently started using the Keto Diet, and the first thing you're told is that bread is forbidden. One slice of bread wipes out an entire day's allowance of carbohydrates.

But you love bread! Don't despair. There is an answer, and *you're absolutely going to love what I have to tell you.*

YOU CAN EAT BREAD ON A KETO DIET!

I ran into the same problem when I first began using the Keto Diet. Low carbs sounded great, but when I began planning my daily meals, I noted that one of my favorite items was completely left off—bread. I've been baking and cooking all my life, so I knew there had to be an answer. I poured through my cookbooks and old recipe cards.

Before long I was holding the answer in my hand. It was an article on alternative flours used in baking. And there were several different types. But the best news is that none of them contained carbohydrates. **They were truly carb-free products.**

I took a trip to my local grocery store and actually found most of them on the shelf in the baking area. The packages were smaller—it's unlikely you're going to find a 20-pound bag of almond flour, even at the health food store. But that's not a problem. Most simple bread recipes call for only a few cups at a time.

So Tasty, You Won't Believe It!

The next question was obvious. What about taste? I admit it took some experimentation. A **lot of the early efforts tasted 'eggy'**. One of the ingredients not found in most non-wheat flours is gluten—the stuff that holds bread together and keeps it from being crumbly. Eggs work as an excellent binder for the alternative flours, but if you use too many, then your bread comes out tasting more of egg than of the flour.

After some additional research, I discovered some very interesting 'natural' binding agents that took care of the eggy-taste problem. Yes! **There ARE good-tasting alternatives to wheat flour bread!**

You've Got to Try It!

Whether you're new to the Keto Diet, or perhaps you've been at it for a while, you really must give these amazing keto bread recipes a try. In fact, you'll be so excited, you'll find yourself wanting to bake every day. Even *your family members who aren't doing the keto diet are going to enjoy your super-tasty keto breads, muffins, bagels, and more!*!!

BASICS OF THE KETO DIET

There's really nothing magical about the Keto Diet. It's based on some simple scientific information about how our body uses the foods that we eat. By controlling what food we put into our bodies, we can improve our health and lower our weight. There may even be benefits to managing diabetes.

Ketosis

Our bodies use the foods we eat to create energy so that we can live. Some foods are easier to convert to energy than others, so naturally, our bodies go after those first. Carbohydrates fall into that category of high-energy foods. Often just called 'carbs', carbohydrates are nutrients we find in starchy foods, such as potatoes, rice, pasta, and bread. Our bodies break down carbohydrates into sugar, which it then burns to give us the energy to get through each day.

One of the key problems with carbs is that if we consume more than we need, our bodies turn them into sugar and then store them as fat in our belly, chest, arms, and legs. So, if we eat too much pasta or too many slices of homemade bread, we end up gaining unwanted weight.

The goal of the Keto Diet is to force your body to burn the fat it already has instead of feeding it more carbohydrates. This is done through the process called Ketosis.

Essentially, ketosis is a metabolic state where our bodies convert all that excess body fat into the sugar we need for daily energy. We can even run a simple test of our urine to see if we are in a state of ketosis. If we are, our bodies produce a byproduct called ketones. By testing our urine with a little strip of treated paper, we can determine if we are in ketosis or not.

Macronutrients

The key to being successful with the Keto Diet is understanding one key concept: macronutrients. There are **three key macronutrients: carbohydrates, proteins, and fats**. By controlling how much of these macronutrients we consume, we can cause our bodies to enter ketosis and begin burning that undesired excess body fat.

Carbohydrates are found in those food items we've already noted above: bread, pasta, rice, and potatoes. There are other sources of carbohydrates, but these are the key items most of us consume on a regular basis.

Proteins are made up of a variety of necessary amino acids. They are found in animal products such as meat, fish, poultry, cheese, and eggs. You do need to be careful not to eat too many proteins, as they too can be turned into unused sugar and our bodies will store them as fat, just as it does with carbohydrates.

Fats are essential to the keto diet and consist largely of oils like those found in avocados and coconuts, nuts such as almonds and walnuts, fish, and various seeds. Some find that increasing their fat content is challenging, but through thoughtful planning, this can be quickly resolved.

By creating a diet that prioritizes our consumption of these macronutrients, we can **encourage our bodies to enter ketosis, thus burning fat and improving our overall health.**

WHY YOU SHOULD COOK KETO BREAD

Keto bread can easily become the answer to being successful following the Keto Diet. It can be a great source of protein and healthy fat, while at the same time minimizing the amounts of carbs you are consuming.

Staying on Track

Let's face it, the problem with any diet is sticking to it. So, when you have simple, go-to foods that you can make every day, staying on track becomes easy. The **more of these delicious keto breads you can put into your daily menu,** the easier it is to monitor your intake of those key macronutrients.

These Keto bread recipes also take into consideration fat and protein content that are an important part of the Keto diet. And don't worry about the sugar you're used to seeing in baked goods at the local shop—some amazing sugar substitutes are completely natural and fit neatly into your diet plan.

Sandwiches

For many of us, lunch is in the form of some type of sandwich. We make sandwiches for our kids to take to school. We put sandwiches in our own lunch for work. When we're home, going to the kitchen and putting together a tasty sandwich is a lunchtime routine.

That doesn't need to change just because you're trying to get healthy and lose weight! While the Keto Diet places some important restrictions on the foods we eat, our lunch-time practice of enjoying sandwiches doesn't need to change. Go ahead and make a sub sandwich with your favorite deli meat and cheese. Add some of your favorite olive oil and don't spare the avocado. You can even sneak some bacon in there if that's your thing.

The point is, using Keto breads for your lunch is a choice you can make without worrying about going off ketosis or blowing all your other diet efforts.

No Guilt

As I said in the introduction, I love bread. Especially homemade. On the Keto Diet, two slices of regular wheat bread can destroy your diet plan for the day. It can kick your body out of ketosis and put you a day behind on your weight-loss goals. But **with Keto bread, you can enjoy it during all three meals and even for dessert.** You might even find some of your coworkers eyeing your homemade bread. Feel free to enjoy it without worrying about your Keto Diet requirements.

It's Easy!

One of the joys of homemade bread is the process of making it! Keto bread is no different. The recipes are simple and easy to follow. You can experiment and add your own flair to bagels, muffins, and holiday treats. Whether you enjoy cooking and baking by yourself, or if you want to include family and friends, these Keto bread recipes are sure to please everyone.

THE ART OF GRAIN-FREE BAKING

In many ways, baking with no-carb flours isn't any different than using wheat-based flour. You can use the same baking equipment as you would in traditional baking without any problems. Learn a few simple basics and you'll be well on your way to creating delicious and satisfying Keto breads.

Basics of Keto Low-Carb Baking at Home

Perhaps the biggest difference to Keto bread making is that the flours used don't contain gluten. Gluten is the binding agent found naturally in wheat flour that helps hold the bread together. Without it, breads become crumbly and don't hold together very well. Finding and using gluten substitutes is an essential part of baking without wheat and other grain-based flours.

Gluten does other things, such as controlling and holding moisture. It also helps with the elastic nature of dough used in bread making. **Finding replacements for gluten becomes one of the biggest challenges.** The good news is that there are several products available.

Solutions for the Main Failures

One of the biggest challenges to grain-free baking is adjusting our own way of thinking about bread baking. You simply **cannot substitute wheat flour one-for-one with an alternative flour.** It simply doesn't work. You can play with changing the ratios of non-wheat flours to get different textures and densities, but don't get discouraged if things don't work out as you hoped.

There are other ingredients that you should avoid using when making Keto bread. Sugar is a definite 'no' on the Keto diet, and unfortunately, many bakers are accustomed to using it generously. Once again, some substitutes work very nicely. In fact, they can be used in traditional baking as well. Learning and experimenting with these sugar alternatives can result in some extremely tasty baked goods that meet the Keto Diet's restrictions.

TIPS FOR PERFECT KETO BREAD BAKING

Baking has always been a great topic for teaching science to children. The reason is simple: baking IS science. There are formulas, measurements, heat control, and altitude and moisture adjustments which all need to be followed for successful outcomes. Baking Keto bread is no different. Here are some great tips to help you be a successful baker in your own home.

Measuring

Cooks often don't make very good bakers because they have grown accustomed to using a pinch of this spice and a dash of that one. But that kind of attitude will get you into trouble in the bakery, especially when working with Keto bread ingredients. **Careful measuring is essential.** If you're experimenting with adding or subtracting the different types of flours, be sure to measure your new ingredient amounts accurately and write them down so that you can repeat or adjust them as necessary. If you don't, you may become disappointed with your outcome.

Temperature

Once again, habits you've developed from using traditional recipes for baking can cause issues when making Keto bread. Strictly follow the recipe's instructions on baking temperature. If you're at a higher altitude, you may need to make some adjustments, but try first what is noted in the recipe.

Storage

As with anything in the kitchen, proper storage is important. Some of the Keto bread flours you will be using need to be stored in air-tight containers. Others might be best stored in the freezer. Avoiding cross-contamination is important as well, so keep your ingredients properly marked and lids tightly secured. You should also write on the package the date it was first opened and used. Some ingredients may have a shorter shelf-life than others.

INGREDIENTS

Good baking requires good ingredients, regardless of who you are baking for. Those who follow a Keto Diet will want to monitor what ingredients they are adding to their recipes. For the preparation of Keto bread, here are some very important ingredients that you will want to have on hand.

Non-Grain Flour

There are two primary flour types used in Keto bread baking: almond flour and coconut flour. Both are excellent choices to work with, and they are readily found in grocery stores around the country. If you ever do have a problem sourcing these, or any other ingredients, most are available online.

Almond flour, as the name suggests, is made from almonds. It is an excellent substitute for wheat flour, and it contains no carbohydrates or gluten. It has a long list of health benefits, and it fits very nicely into the Keto Diet regimen.

Coconut flour comes from grinding dried coconut and contains a wide range of healthful nutrients. As with almond flour, there are no carbs in coconut flour, and it is also gluten-free. It does give a slight coconut taste to baked goods, but most find it very pleasant and agreeable.

Binding Agents

As noted above, the gluten commonly found in wheat bread is what keeps it together. Because neither almond nor coconut flour contain gluten, bread baked with them crumbles and falls apart easily. Adding a simple binding agent solves that problem easily.

Psyllium husk powder is an excellent choice. Made from the Plantago plant, it is an excellent source of fiber, and it works very nicely as a binding agent. It also helps hold moisture, so is a real benefit in making Keto bread.

Flax seeds also serve as both a binder and as a source of dietary fiber.

Eggs, too, are a natural binding agent for baking. They can help increase protein in a Keto Diet and work well in holding together breads and baked goods. Too many eggs, though, can cause your bread to have an 'eggy' taste that might overpower the other flavors.

Nut Flours

Almond flour leads the list of nut flours, but others are becoming more popular. Next in line is pecan flour. Because it is milled with its husk still in place, the final product tends to be darker in color. If you're looking for a white bread appearance, pecan flour may not be your first choice.

Two other nut flours which have similar darker appearances are hazelnut and walnut. Hazelnut flour has been popular in Europe for quite some time and is only now becoming available in the US. Walnut flour has a stronger taste that adds a distinctive flavor to baked goods. Both can be made by grinding the nuts in a food processor.

Fats and Oils

Some Keto bread recipes call for oil in their preparation. Fortunately, fats and oils are a key part of the Keto Diet, so using them in baked goods is an excellent idea. Perhaps the oil with the highest fat content is **avocado oil**. It is useful in most recipes and doesn't influence the taste of the products. Olive oil and coconut oil both work well in baking. **Coconut oil** does have a stronger taste, which may influence the outcome of your baking.

SUGAR SUBSTITUTES

Sugar is used throughout cooking and baking, but for those on a strict Keto Diet, it's to be avoided at all costs. Most of the sugars we are used to are highly refined and can cause serious problems in maintaining ketosis. There are, however, some readily available and very delightful substitutes.

- First on the list is Stevia. It comes in both a powdered and liquid form, which makes it useful in a variety of applications. It comes from a herb called "sugar leaf" and contains no measurable calories or nutrients. It does, however, taste very sweet.

- Another favorite sweetener is monk fruit. It contains no carbohydrates and is reported to be 250 times sweeter than regular sugar. It's noted that monk fruit sweetener helps to release the body's natural insulin to control sugar in the bloodstream.

- Erythritol is a sugar alcohol and is a popular sugar substitute. It is less likely to cause problems with the digestive system than other sugar alcohols.

- Xylitol is another sugar alcohol. It is very useful as a sweetener, but some people find it upsets their digestive system.

BASIC KETO BREAD

Picnic bread

Tartar bread

Turmeric bread

Almond coconut bread

Sour cream bread

Flaxseed bread

PICNIC BREAD

Servings: 12 slices | Prep Time: 10 minutes | Cooking Time: 1 hour

Ingredients:

- 2 cups (225 g) almond flour
- ¼ cup (60 ml) lukewarm water
- 4 whole eggs
- 1 Tbsp. sesame oil/ghee
- 1 Tbsp. xanthan gum
- 1 Tbsp. sweetener of your choice
- 1 Tbsp. apple cider vinegar
- ½ tsp. kosher salt
- 1 tsp. low carb baking powder
- ½ tsp. baking soda
- 2 tsp. instant yeast

Steps:

1. Preheat your oven to 350°F (180°C). Grease (with cooking spray) an 8"x4" bread tin and set it aside for later use.
2. In a bowl, add the yeast to warm water and stir to eliminate any clumps. This is best done with a fork. Set aside.
3. While the yeast is working away, combine baking powder, baking soda, salt, xanthan gum, and sweetener.
4. Combine with eggs, avocado oil/butter, and apple cider vinegar. Mix everything with an electric mixer until smooth.
5. Add the yeast along with the warm water. Continue mixing with your mixer for about one more minute. This will ensure extra air incorporation into your dough to make your bread fluffier.
6. Transfer the dough into your prepared pan and bake for one hour or until your toothpick comes out clean.
7. Allow cooling completely before cutting and serving. Keep it fresh in the fridge for up to one week, or freeze for up to three months.

Baking Tip:

- This bread will look like it is burning after the first 30 minutes, do not panic! The inside needs more time to firm up, and the dark exterior keeps moisture in.

Nutritional Facts (Per Serving):

Calories 118, Fat 10 g, Carbohydrates 4 g, Protein 4 g

TARTAR BREAD

Servings: 12 slices | Prep Time: 15 minutes | Cooking Time: 30 minutes

Ingredients:

- 1½ cups (170 g) almond flour
- 6 large eggs (whites and yolks)
- ¼ cup (60 g) unsalted butter, melted
- ¼ tsp. kosher salt
- 3 tsp. low carb baking powder
- 1 tsp. unsalted butter, for greasing
- ¼ Tbsp. cream of tartar
- 6 drops of liquid Stevia (can be replaced with erythritol)

Steps:

1. Preheat the oven to 375°F (190°C) and grease an 8"x 4" loaf tin with butter.
2. Separate the egg whites from the yolks into two separate bowls. Add cream of tartar to the egg whites and beat with a whisk (or electric whisk) until the whites are pearl white and stiff peaks form when the whisk is lifted.
3. In a food processor, combine egg yolks, melted butter, almond flour, baking powder, salt, and ⅓ of your egg whites. Mix this until thoroughly combined. The mixture will be lumpy until the remaining egg whites are added! Add Stevia and mix until incorporated.
4. Add the remaining egg whites and mix until just combined. Be careful not to overmix, as this will result in a denser texture and a smaller loaf.
5. Transfer the bread batter into the prepared tin. Bake for 30 minutes.
6. Check for doneness with a toothpick. If it comes out clean, your loaf is done!
7. Allow to cool properly before serving, and store in the refrigerator for up to 10 days.

<u>Baking Tip:</u>

- I recommend you test your loaf with a toothpick after 30 minutes of baking.

Nutritional Facts (Per Serving):

Calories 90, Fat 7 g, Carbohydrates 2 g, Protein 3 g

TURMERIC BREAD

Servings: 8 | Prep Time: 5 minutes | Cooking Time: 22 minutes

Ingredients:

- 2 cups (225 g) almond flour
- 3 large eggs
- ¼ cup (60 g) unsalted butter, melted
- ¼ cup granulated sweetener of your choice
- ½ tsp. turmeric
- ¼ tsp. kosher salt
- ½ tsp. baking soda

Steps:

1. Lightly oil an 8"x8" bread pan. Set aside.
2. Turn your oven to 350°F (180°C) and leave to preheat.
3. Mix flour, sweetener, salt, turmeric, and baking soda in a large bowl. Add in butter and eggs, and mix until fully combined.
4. Pour your bread batter into your prepared pan.
5. Place on the middle shelf of your oven and bake for 20–22 minutes. The surface should be beautifully golden, and a toothpick inserted into the middle should come out clean.
6. Allow cooling completely before cutting and serving.
7. This bread can last in the refrigerator for up to three days, or you can place it in a freezer-friendly bag and freeze for up to four months.

Baking Tip:

- If you notice your batter is too thick, add some moisture. Water is the best method to do this. Start with 2 tablespoons and add as needed.

Nutritional Facts (Per Serving):

Calories 133, Fat 8 g, Carbohydrates 4 g, Protein 4 g

ALMOND COCONUT BREAD

Servings: 12 | Prep Time: 5 minutes | Cooking Time: 45 minutes

Ingredients:

- ¾ cup (65 g) coconut flour
- ½ cup (120 ml) organic almond milk
- 6 large eggs
- ½ cup (120 ml) coconut oil
- 1 Tbsp. sweetener
- ¼ tsp. kosher salt
- 1½ tsp. low carb baking powder

Steps:

1. Grease an 8"x 4" loaf tin and set the oven temperature to 375°F (190°C).
2. Beat eggs in a bowl until combined. Add almond milk, coconut oil, and honey. Mix until well combined.
3. Add coconut flour, salt, and baking powder to the mixture. Mix until just combined. Don't over mix your mixture!
4. Pour the bread batter into your prepared tin, and smooth it out. Make sure your batter is level.
5. Bake for 45 minutes or until your toothpick comes out clean when inserted into the thickest point of your loaf.
6. Allow cooling completely before serving. Store in the refrigerator for up to 1 week. Freezer friendly.

<u>Baking Tips:</u>

- For a savory loaf, leave out the sweetener and add spices.
- For a sweeter loaf, add an extra tablespoon of your favorite sweetener.

Nutritional Facts (Per Serving):

Calories 266, Fat 21.3 g, Carbohydrates 11.7 g, Protein 8.1 g

SOUR CREAM BREAD

Servings: 10 slices | Prep Time: 10 minutes | Cooking Time: 25 minutes

Ingredients:

- 1¼ cups (140 g) almond flour
- 2 Tbsp. coconut flour
- 2 large eggs
- 3 Tbsp. of sour cream
- ½ Tbsp. erythritol
- ½ Tbsp. apple cider vinegar
- ⅛ tsp. kosher salt
- 1 tsp. baking soda
- 1 tsp. low carb baking powder

Steps:

1. Preheat the oven to 350°F (180°C) and grease your skillet. Set aside.
2. Mix baking soda, baking powder, coconut flour, almond flour, erythritol, and salt in a bowl until well blended.
3. Whisk eggs together and add to the bowl. Add apple cider vinegar and sour cream, and mix well until the wet ingredients are incorporated with the dry, and no clumps remain.
4. Create a round ball of dough with your hands, and place it into your skillet. Score the top lightly with a knife, how you prefer. I recommend an X.
5. Place in the oven and bake for 25–28 minutes, or until your toothpick comes out clean.
6. Set aside to cool completely in the skillet before serving. Keep this bread fresh by storing it in the refrigerator for up to a week.

Jennifer Tip:

- Raisins or cranberries work well with this bread.

Nutritional Facts (Per Serving):

Calories 112, Fat 8.5 g, Carbohydrates 6.5 g, Protein 4.6 g

FLAXSEED BREAD

Servings: 15 slices | Prep Time: 15 minutes | Cooking Time: 30 minutes

Ingredients:

- 2 cups (300 g) ground flaxseed
- 5 whole eggs
- ½ cup (120 ml) lukewarm water
- 5 Tbsp. coconut oil
- 2 Tbsp. apple cider vinegar
- 1 tsp. kosher salt
- 1 Tbsp. low carb baking powder

Steps:

1. Preheat the oven to 350°F (180°C) and grease your 8"x4" loaf pan. Set aside.
2. Whisk egg whites until they are pearl white, form stiff peaks when the whisk is lifted and set aside. In a separate bowl, mix baking powder, flaxseed, oil, and salt together.
3. Add water, egg yolks, and apple cider vinegar to the mixture.
4. Gently fold the beaten egg yolks into the flaxseed mixture.
5. Pour the batter into the pan and bake for 30 minutes or until a toothpick comes out clean.
6. Allow cooling completely before serving. The loaf can last in the fridge for up to 1 week.

<u>Baking Tip:</u>

- To dress up your loaf, I recommend adding dried vegetables, seeds, or spices.

Nutritional Facts (Per Serving):

Calories 340, Fat 8 g, Carbohydrates 10 g, Protein 14 g

ENERGY LUNCH BREAD

Delicate Zucchini Bread

Herb Bread

Mozzarella Balls

Cranberry Loaf

Ginger Spicy Bread

Cocoa Bread

DELICATE ZUCCHINI BREAD

Servings: 12 slices | Prep Time: 10 minutes | Cooking Time: 50 minutes

Ingredients:

- 1¼ cup (140 g) almond flour
- ¼ cup + 3 Tbsp. (50 g) coconut flour
- 4 whole eggs
- 1½ cup (230 g) shredded zucchini
- ½ cup (100 g) softened butter
- ¼ cup (30 g) chopped pecans
- 1 tsp. vanilla extract
- 3 Tbsp. erythritol
- ½ tsp. nutmeg
- 1 tsp. cinnamon
- 1½ tsp. low carb baking powder

Steps:

1. Preheat your oven to 355°F (180°C) and line a bread pan with parchment paper. Set aside.
2. Squeeze out as much water as possible from your shredded zucchini by wrapping it in a kitchen towel or cheesecloth and wringing it. Set the zucchini aside, covered.
3. With an electric mixer, beat your eggs until frothy and lighter in color. The eggs should also almost double. Add butter and vanilla, and mix again until incorporated.
4. Mix your zucchini into your egg mixture before adding all your dry ingredients and mixing until a cohesive dough is formed.
5. Transfer your dough to the bread pan after mixing in half of the pecans.
6. Top your dough with the remaining nuts.
7. Slide the dough into the preheated oven and bake for 50 minutes.
8. Allow to cool completely, and store in the refrigerator for up to four days.

<u>Baking Tips</u>

- Substitute pecans for any nuts of your choice.

Nutritional Facts (Per Serving):

Calories 180, Fat 16.5 g, Carbohydrates 4.6 g, Protein 6 g

HERB BREAD

Servings: 10 slices | Prep Time: 1¾ hours | Cooking Time: ¾ hour

Ingredients:

- 2 cups (200 g) almond flour
- ¾ cup (90 g) arrowroot powder
- ⅓ cup + 3 Tbsp. (125 ml) warm water
- 2 large eggs, separated
- 2 tsp. erythritol
- 1 tsp. xanthan gum
- 2 tsp. minced garlic
- ¼ tsp. pepper
- 2 tsp. rosemary
- 1 tsp. dried thyme
- 1 Tbsp. olive oil
- ¼ tsp. kosher salt
- 1½ tsp. instant yeast
- 1 cup water as needed

Steps:

1. Grease a bread pan and set it aside.
2. In a large bowl, mix together the two flours, xanthan gum, yeast, and sugar, mix until well combined, and proceed to add rosemary, oregano, garlic, salt, and pepper. Mix once more.
3. Add the egg whites and ⅓ cup of warm water. Mix until all is well incorporated.
4. If the dough appears too dry, add more water to the mixture.
5. Shape the dough into a loaf shape, then place in the bread pan.
6. Put your yolks into a small bowl along with a little bit of pepper. Mix with a whisk until they are combined, and gently brush the top of your bread dough with it.
7. Cover your dough and let it rise for 1½ hours. Meanwhile, preheat your oven to 400°F (205°C).
8. Once your dough has risen, cover it with tin foil and bake it for 30 minutes. After 30 minutes, uncover your dough and bake for a further 15 minutes. This process will ensure a soft center and a crispy exterior.
9. You can keep this bread in an air-tight container for up to a week.

<u>Baking Tip</u>

- Covering the bread with tin foil ensures less browning during cooking.

Nutritional Facts (Per Serving):

Calories 127, Fat 9 g, Carbohydrates 9.1 g, Protein 4.1 g

MOZZARELLA BALLS

Servings: 16 balls | Prep Time: 10 minutes | Cooking Time: 10 minutes

Ingredients:

- ¾ cup (85 g) almond flour
- 1½ cups (180 g) mozzarella cheese
- ½ cup (45 g) grated parmesan
- 2 Tbsp. cream cheese
- ½ cup crumbled queso fresco
- 1 whole egg, beaten
- 2 tsp. low carb baking powder

Steps:

1. Put your oven to 400°F (205°C) and line a baking sheet with parchment paper.
2. Melt cream cheese and mozzarella together in a microwave. Mix until fully combined.
3. Add in the parmesan, flour, and baking powder. Mix again before adding the beaten egg and forming a dough with your hands.
4. Next, add in the crumbled queso fresco and evenly distribute it in the dough. The cheese won't melt into the dough, so make sure it is evenly spread out.
5. With your hands, make 16 golf ball-sized balls and place them an inch apart on the baking sheet you have prepared earlier.
6. Place these in the oven and bake for 10 minutes until they turn a golden color. Serve after cooling completely.
7. Keeping the container air-tight for up to five days will keep the ingredients fresh.

Baking Tip

- For an extra pop of flavor, sprinkle cheese on top of your rolls.

Nutritional Facts (Per Serving):

Calories 260, Fat 18.5 g, Carbohydrates 9.8 g, Protein 20 g

CRANBERRY LOAF

Servings: 10 slices | Prep Time: 15 minutes | Cooking Time: 1 hour

Ingredients:

- 1 cup (85 g) coconut flour
- 1 cup (150 g) fresh cranberries
- ½ cup (120 ml) water
- ½ cup (120 ml) coconut oil, melted
- 3 egg whites
- 3 whole eggs
- ½ cup (40 g) shredded coconut
- ½ cup (100 g) erythritol (or sweetener of your choice)
- ½ tsp. vanilla extract
- 1 tsp. coconut extract
- ¼ tsp. kosher salt
- 2 tsp. low carb baking powder

Steps:

1. Preheat your oven to 350°F (180°C) and grease an 8"x 4" tin. Set aside.
2. Whisk together the shredded coconut, sweetener, flour, baking powder, and salt.
3. Add coconut oil, eggs, and egg whites, as well as lemon and vanilla extract, and mix until homogeneous. Stir in the water to create a smooth dough.
4. At this point, mix in most of your blueberries. Leave some out for topping your loaf. Once your blueberries are mixed in, transfer your dough to the prepared tin.
5. Top your loaf with the leftover blueberries and place it in the oven.
6. Cook for 50 minutes, or until a toothpick is clean when inserted.
7. Allow the loaf to cool inside the tin completely before serving.

<u>Baking Tip</u>

- Feel free to substitute the blueberries for your favorite berry.

Nutritional Facts (Per Serving):

Calories 174, Fat 13.9 g, Carbohydrates 7.3 g, Protein 5.2 g

GINGER SPICY BREAD

Servings: 12 slices | Prep Time: 15 minutes | Cooking Time: 30 minutes

Ingredients:

Bread Batter:

- ¾ cup (90 g) coconut flour
- ¼ cup (60 g) butter, melted
- 4 whole eggs
- 1 tsp. vanilla extract
- ¾ cup (150 g) erythritol
- 2 Tbsp. gingerbread spice mix
- 1 tsp. low carb baking powder

Gingerbread Spice Mix:

- ¼ tsp. kosher salt
- 2 tsp. cinnamon
- 2 tsp. ginger
- ½ tsp. allspice
- ½ tsp. nutmeg
- ½ tsp. ground clove

Steps:

1. Heat the oven to 350°F (180°C) and line a loaf tin with baking parchment. Set aside.
2. Whisk together eggs, melted (but cooled!) butter, and vanilla until homogeneous, bubbly, and lighter in color.
3. Add in baking powder, flour, and sweetener. Mix again until fully combined.
4. Next, add your gingerbread spice mix and incorporate it into your batter.
5. Pour the batter into your prepared pan and bake for about 25–30 minutes.
6. Optionally, sprinkle some walnuts on top of your loaf before placing it in the oven.
7. Allow to cool fully in the tin before taking out and serving.
8. The product should be stored in an air-tight container for four days.

<u>Baking Tip</u>

- Make sure your melted butter is cooled, so it does not scramble your eggs.

Nutritional Facts (Per Serving):

Calories 249, Fat 22 g, Carbohydrates 3.7 g, Protein 3.9 g

COCOA BREAD

Servings: 10 slices | Prep Time: 10 minutes | Cooking Time: 50 minutes

Ingredients:

- 1¼ cups (140 g) almond flour
- 1 oz. (30 g) baking chocolate, melted
- 3 oz. (85 g) cream cheese
- 4 whole eggs
- 4 Tbsp. butter
- 1 tsp. instant coffee
- ¼ cup (25 g) cocoa powder
- ¾ cup (180 g) erythritol (or your choice of sweetener)
- ¼ tsp. kosher salt
- 1½ tsp. low carb baking powder

Steps:

1. Preheat the oven to 350°F (180°C) and grease a loaf tin. Set aside.
2. Mix flour, coffee, cocoa powder, baking powder, and salt in a large bowl and set aside once fully incorporated.
3. With an electric mixer, beat together butter and the sweetener of your choice until the ingredients are entirely homogeneous and the butter appears fluffy and light in color. Next, add in the cream cheese and mix once more to incorporate.
4. One by one, add in your eggs, mixing your batter each time, and making sure the eggs are fully mixed before adding the next.
5. Gradually add your dry ingredients until all are in the same bowl and your batter has no more lumps.
6. Now, add in your melted chocolate and combine it with your batter. Pour your batter into your prepared tin and place it in the oven.
7. Bake for 50 minutes until firm to the touch and your toothpick comes out completely clean.
8. Let your loaf cool for 30 minutes in the tin before transferring it onto a cooling rack to cool completely.
9. Store in an air-tight container for up to one week.

<u>Baking Tip</u>

- Stir in some white chocolate chunks for a double chocolate loaf.

Nutritional Facts (Per Serving):

Calories 175, Fat 8.4 g, Carbohydrates 4.7 g, Protein 6.2 g

CRISPY MEDITERRANEAN LOAVES

Provence Bread

Italian Ciabatta

French Baguettes

Cheese Bread

Rosemary Focaccia with Olives

Vegetable Flatbread

Italian Biscotti with Berries

Almond Cookies

PROVENCE BREAD

Servings: 12 slices | Prep Time: 20 minutes | Cooking Time: 1 hour

Ingredients:

- 1½ cup (170 g) almond flour
- 5 Tbsp. ground flaxseed
- 2 Tbsp. psyllium husk powder
- ½ cup (120 ml) sour cream
- 4 large eggs
- ½ cup (120 ml) olive oil
- 1.7 oz. (50 g) chopped olives
- 2 Tbsp. apple cider vinegar
- 1 tsp. dried, ground rosemary
- 1 tsp. dried basil
- 1 tsp. kosher salt
- 1 tsp. baking soda

Steps:

1. In a large bowl, combine almond flour, baking soda, flaxseed, rosemary, psyllium husk powder, salt, and set aside.

2. In another large bowl, beat the eggs for five minutes until bubbly and light. Gradually and slowly start adding olive oil to the mixture, which will create a smooth emulsion. When all the oil has been added, proceed to slowly add sour cream and apple cider vinegar. Keep beating with an electric mixer. The secret to this loaf is to overmix the wet ingredients ever so slightly.

3. Gradually, add the previously mixed dry ingredients to the wet mixture. As the dough will become more difficult to mix, it may be a good idea to switch to the dough hook in a stand mixer. If mixing with an electric mixer, switch to your hands.

4. Finally, add the chopped olives to your dough and mix them in. Cover your dough and let it rest for 15 minutes at room temperature.

5. In the meantime, preheat your oven to 390°F (200°C) and grease your bread pan, preferably with olive oil or coconut oil.

6. Transfer your bread to the bread pan and bake for 30 minutes. After those 30 minutes, reduce the temperature to 300°F (150°C) and bake for another 30 minutes.

7. Allow the bread to cool completely in the pan before serving. You can store this in the refrigerator or freezer for up to four months in an air-tight container.

<u>Baking Tips</u>

- Sprinkle some seeds on top of your bread. I recommend going with flax seeds.

Nutritional Facts (Per Serving):

Calories 150, Fat 14 g, Carbohydrates 3 g, Protein 3 g

ITALIAN CIABATTA

Servings: 2 rolls | Prep Time: 2 hours | Cooking Time: 40 minutes

Ingredients:

- 1 cup (110 g) superfine almond flour
- 1 cup vital wheat gluten
- ¼ cup (40 g) flaxseed meal
- ½ cup + 2 Tbsp. (140 ml) warm water
- 1 Tbsp. butter, melted
- 3 Tbsp. extra virgin olive oil
- 1 tsp. sugar
- ¾ tsp. kosher salt
- 2¼ tsp. active dry yeast
- 1½ tsp. low carb baking powder

Steps:

1. Prepare a baking sheet with parchment paper.
2. Mix ½ cup of warm water, sugar, and yeast together in a bowl, then cover and allow to sit until bubbles rise to the surface and the mixture appears foamy.
3. In a large bowl, combine almond flour, wheat gluten, flaxseed meal, salt, and baking powder.
4. Add olive oil and remaining water to the yeast mixture and transfer to your mixed dry ingredients. Mix well until a wet dough is formed.
5. Knead this dough for a further three minutes, but don't overmix it.
6. Separate this dough into two separate pieces and form it into short cylinder shapes. They should be 2½" x 7" in size. Transfer them onto your prepared baking sheet.
7. Preheat your oven to 110°F (45°C), and turn it off. Place your dough into the warm oven and leave to rise for up to one hour. After your dough has risen, take the loaves back out and preheat your oven to 350°F (180°C).
8. Brush your loaves with the melted butter and place in the preheated oven for 40 minutes. As your loaves are baking, brush them with butter every 10 to 15 minutes.
9. Allow your loaves to cool completely on the baking sheet after taking them out of the oven.

<u>Baking Tip</u>

- For an extra burst of flavor, sprinkle the top of your ciabatta loaves with parmesan cheese.

Nutritional Facts (Per Serving):

Calories 286, Fat 19 g, Carbohydrates 9 g, Protein 21 g

FRENCH BAGUETTES

Servings: 8 baguettes | Prep Time: ¼ hour | Cooking Time: ½ - ¾ hour

Ingredients:

- 1½ cup (150 g) almond flour
- ½ cup (60 g) coconut flour
- ½ cup (750 g) flax meal
- ⅓ cup (40 g) psyllium husk powder
- 6 egg whites
- 2 large whole eggs
- ¾ cup (180 ml) buttermilk
- 1 cup (240 ml) lukewarm water
- ¼ cup (60 ml) white wine vinegar
- 1 tsp. kosher salt
- 1 tsp. baking soda

Steps:

1. Put parchment paper on a baking sheet and preheat the oven to 400°F (205°C). Set the sheet aside.
2. Mix almond flour, coconut flour, psyllium husk, flax meal, baking soda, and salt in a large bowl. Set aside.
3. In another bowl, combine buttermilk, two whole eggs, and the egg whites. Add this mixture to your dry ingredients and mix until a smooth dough has formed.
4. Add in the white wine vinegar and water. Continue mixing until just combined.
5. Form eight baguettes from the dough and place them on your prepared baking sheet. Leave space between each of them, as they will rise and expand.
6. Bake for 10 minutes at the set temperature, then reduce this temperature to 340°F (170°C), continuing to bake for another 30 minutes.
7. Allow cooling completely on the baking sheet before serving. Refrigerate for up to 1 week, or freeze for up to 3 months.

Baking Tips:

- Add all dry ingredients to a Ziploc bag and mix them together to save time. Then all you need to do is add my wet ingredients. Make sure to label the Ziploc bags with the date of packaging.

Nutritional Facts (Per Serving):

Calories 232, Fat 16.4 g, Carbohydrates 4.5 g, Protein 12.5 g

CHEESE BREAD

Servings: 10 slices | Prep Time: ¼ hour | Cooking Time: 1 hour

Ingredients:

- 2 cups (225 g) almond flour
- 7 large eggs
- ⅓ cup (80 g) unsalted butter, melted
- ½ tsp. Xanthan Gum
- ¼ cup (20 g) shredded Parmesan cheese
- 2 Tbsp. olive oil
- 2 tsp. dried / fresh basil
- 1 tsp. dried / fresh oregano
- ½ tsp. garlic powder
- ½ tsp. onion powder
- ½ tsp. kosher salt
- 1 tsp. low carb baking powder

Steps:

1. Preheat the oven to 350°F (180°C) and prepare a 9"x 5" baking pan by lining it with parchment paper.
2. Beat the eggs until lighter and foaming. Add olive oil and melted butter, and mix until homogeneous.
3. Add flour, xanthan gum, parmesan, and all your seasonings to the mixture, and softly fold with a spatula until all are combined.
4. Pour this batter into your prepared tin and bake for 45 to 50 minutes or until a toothpick inserted in the center comes out clean.
5. Allow to cool for an hour in the pan before taking it out and placing the loaf on a wire rack to cool completely.
6. Refrigerate for up to five days.

<u>Baking Tips</u>

- This loaf makes an excellent buttered toast!

Nutritional Facts (Per Serving):

Calories 191, Fat 12 g, Carbohydrates 3.8 g, Protein 6.1 g

ROSEMARY FOCACCIA WITH OLIVES

Servings: 10 | Prep Time: 15 minutes | Cooking Time: 25 minutes

Ingredients:

- 3 cups (340 g) almond flour
- ½ cup (120 ml) almond milk
- 5 large eggs, separated
- ½ cup (30 g) sun-dried tomatoes
- ½ cup (90 g) olives
- 1 Tbsp. extra virgin olive oil
- 1 tsp. apple cider vinegar
- 1 tsp. kosher salt
- 2 tsp. low carb baking powder
- 1 Tbsp. chopped rosemary, for sprinkling

Steps:

1. Prepare a 9"x13" baking sheet with parchment paper and preheat the oven to 350°F (180°C).
2. Combine salt, baking powder, and almond flour in a large bowl and mix until well combined.
3. Beat one egg and add together with almond milk and apple cider vinegar to the flour mixture. Mix well until a smooth dough forms. Set aside to rest.
4. Separate whites from yolks in the four remaining eggs. With an electric mixer, mix egg whites until fluffy, white, and stiff peaks form.
5. Add your egg whites to the flour mixture and gently fold, being careful not to deflate the eggs.
6. Gently spoon your dough onto the prepared baking sheet. Add sun-dried tomatoes, olives, and drizzle with extra virgin olive oil.
7. Bake for 20-25 minutes. The focaccia should be lightly golden at the end of baking. Allow cooling completely before taking out of the baking sheet and serving.
8. Keep in the refrigerator for up to five days in an air-tight container.

Baking Tip:

- You can make your focaccia a dessert by topping it with peaches or apples!

Nutritional Facts (Per Serving):

Calories 134, Fat 12 g, Carbohydrates 3.1 g, Protein 4.4 g

VEGETABLE FLATBREAD

Servings: 8 | Prep Time: 10 minutes | Cooking Time: 25 minutes

Ingredients:

- 2 cups (225 g) almond flour
- 1 cup (130 g) arrowroot flour
- 2 cups (200 g) cauliflower florets
- 1 whole egg
- 2 cloves of garlic
- 2 Tbsp. olive oil
- 1 tsp. kosher salt

Steps:

1. Prepare a baking sheet with parchment paper and preheat the oven to 350°F (180°C).
2. Boil the cauliflower florets until soft for about five minutes, and drain. Transfer to a food processor and process until finely chopped.
3. Scrape down the sides of the food processor and add the egg and garlic. Process again until fully combined.
4. Next, add almond flour, arrowroot flour, and salt. Process until everything is combined, taking care to scrape down the sides as necessary.
5. Transfer the mixture to your prepared baking sheet and spread it into your desired shape (I always go with an oval).
6. Drizzle your dough with olive oil and bake for 20 minutes until golden brown.
7. If you are either keeping it plain or not using it immediately, store it in the refrigerator after it cools completely on the baking sheet for up to three days.

<u>Baking Tips</u>

- I like topping this bread with a mixture of tomatoes, eggplant, pesto, and fresh mozzarella.

Nutritional Facts (Per Serving):

Calories 155, Fat 11.9 g, Carbohydrates 8.3 g, Protein 5.4 g

ITALIAN BISCOTTI WITH BERRIES

Servings: 8 biscotti | Prep Time: ¼ hour | Cooking Time: 1 hour

Ingredients:

- 1½ cup (170 g) almond flour
- 2 Tbsp. arrowroot flour
- 2 large eggs
- ½ cup (70 g) whole almonds
- ½ cup (60 g) dried cranberries
- ⅓ cup (70 g) granular Swerve sweetener
- One lemon, zested
- 1 tsp. vanilla
- ¼ tsp. kosher salt
- ½ tsp. baking soda

Steps:

1. Set your oven to 350°F (180°C) and line a baking sheet with parchment paper.
2. Combine lemon zest, vanilla, sweetener, and eggs together in a bowl, and mix until frothy with an electric mixer.
3. To the lemon zest mixture, add flour, salt, baking soda, and mix until well until a dough forms. Add almonds and cranberries to this dough and incorporate it evenly.
4. Transfer your dough to the prepared baking sheet in a long rectangle. Bake for 20 minutes until they are nicely golden brown.
5. Take them out and let them cool for one hour. After they have cooled significantly, cut the dough into long strips and at a small angle.
6. Put these in the oven for another 15 to 20 minutes. This will give them that extra crunch.
7. Allow these biscotti to cool entirely before serving. The best way to keep these fresh is to refrigerate them for up to a week.

Baking Tip

- White chocolate and macadamia nuts go well in this recipe too!

Nutritional Facts (Per Serving):

Calories 173, Fat 10 g, Carbohydrates 17 g, Protein 5 g

ALMOND COOKIES

Servings: 20 – 24 cookies | Prep Time: 20 minutes | Cooking Time: 20 minutes

Ingredients:

- 1½ cups (170 g) almond flour
- ½ cup (100 g) erythritol
- 24 almonds (25 g)
- 1 whole egg
- 1 tsp. lemon extract
- 1 Tbsp. lemon zest

Steps:

1. Set your oven to 350°F (180°C) and line a baking dish with parchment paper.
2. With an electric mixer, beat the eggs. Add the zest, flour, extract, and erythritol. Mix with your hand until a smooth dough forms.
3. Using a tablespoon to measure out the cookies, form each cookie into an oval shape and place it on your baking sheet. You should make 24 cookies. Take care to make sure all are uniform.
4. Firmly press an almond into each of the cookies until it is securely sitting on top of the cookie dough.
5. Bake your cookies for 20 minutes and let them cool completely before serving.
6. These can be stored in an air-tight container for up to one week. I don't recommend freezing these cookies, however!

<u>Baking Tip</u>

- If you like your cookies a little bit zesty, add more lemon extract.

Nutritional Facts (Per Serving):

Calories 48, Fat 1.6 g, Carbohydrates 10 g, Protein 0.9 g

NUTRITIOUS PIZZA AND TORTILLAS

Keto Pizza Base

Cheddar Pizza Crust

Calzone Pizza

Keto Tortillas

Green Tortillas

KETO PIZZA BASE

Servings: 8 slices | Prep Time: 10 minutes | Cooking Time: 20 minutes

Ingredients:

- 2½ cups (280 g) almond flour
- 2 whole eggs, beaten
- ¼ cup (60 ml) extra virgin olive oil
- ½ tsp. garlic powder
- ¼ tsp. onion powder
- ½ tsp. kosher salt
- ½ tsp. baking soda
- ½ tsp. active dry yeast

Steps:

1. Bake the muffins at 400°F (205°C) and line a baking sheet with parchment paper.
2. Mix together baking soda, salt, garlic and onion powders, and yeast.
3. Make a dent in the center and add the beaten eggs and olive oil to the dent.
4. Combine with a wooden spoon, then knead with your hands until a smooth dough forms.
5. Place the dough onto your prepared baking sheet and form it into a round disk.
6. Place your pizza base into the oven and bake for 10 to 12 minutes.
7. After that, take your dough out and top it with your desired toppings.
8. Place your pizza back into the oven for the remaining 8 to 10 minutes or until the cheese has melted and is just starting to bubble.
9. Serve while hot.

Baking Tips

- Pre-baking your crust ensures that it is cooked throughout!

Nutritional Facts (Per Serving):

Calories 229, Fat 21 g, Carbohydrates 6 g, Protein 7 g

CHEDDAR PIZZA CRUST

Servings: 8 slices | Prep Time: 10 minutes | Cooking Time: 20 minutes

Ingredients:

- 1 cup (110 g) almond flour
- 1 cup (90 g) shredded cheddar
- 2 Tbsp. cottage cheese
- 2 large eggs
- 2 Tbsp. butter, melted and cooled
- ½ tsp. garlic powder
- ¼ tsp. kosher salt

Steps:

1. Prepare the oven by heating it to 400°F (205°C) and line a baking sheet with parchment paper.
2. Whisk together cottage cheese, eggs, and melted butter. Set aside.
3. In a large bowl, combine flour, salt, garlic powder, and shredded cheddar. Mix to combine.
4. Next, add the wet ingredients to your dry ingredients and stir until homogenous. Your mixture will be lumpy.
5. Place your dough on a piece of parchment paper and put another piece of parchment paper on top. Roll your dough out into a rectangular piece and transfer it onto your prepared baking sheet.
6. Place in the oven for 14 minutes or until the crust is a lightly golden brown.
7. Place all of your toppings on top of your crust, and place it back in the oven for six minutes or until your cheese has melted and is slightly bubbling.
8. Serve while hot.

Baking Tip

- You can substitute sour cream for cottage cheese 1:1.

Nutritional Facts (Per Serving):

Calories 434, Fat 38 g, Carbohydrates 7 g, Protein 17 g

CALZONE PIZZA

Servings: 4 calzones | Prep Time: ¼ hour | Cooking Time: 20 minutes

Ingredients:

- 1½ cups (170 g) almond flour
- 1¼ cups (140 g) shredded mozzarella
- 3 oz. (90 g) pepperoni, cubed
- ½ tsp. xanthan gum
- ¾ tsp. Italian seasoning
- ⅛ tsp. garlic powder
- ¼ cup (60 g) pizza sauce
- 3 Tbsp. water
- 1 Tbsp. olive oil

Steps:

1. Place parchment paper on a baking sheet and preheat the oven to 375°F (190°C). Set aside.
2. Mix together Italian seasoning, flour, and garlic powder until thoroughly combined, then add olive oil and water.
3. Knead with your hands until a smooth dough forms. Divide this dough into four equally sized balls.
4. Roll the balls out between two sheets of parchment paper until you have four circles around six inches in diameter each.
5. Spread pizza sauce on your circles like you would on a pizza base. Then, on just half the dough, place your pepperoni and mozzarella cheese.
6. Carefully fold your calzones and fold the edges tightly over each other to form a seal.
7. Place them in the oven for 15 minutes until lightly golden.
8. Serve while hot.

Baking Tip

- Experiment with calzone fillings, the world's your oyster!

Nutritional Facts (Per Serving):

Calories 286, Fat 26 g, Carbohydrates 7.7 g, Protein 9 g

KETO TORTILLAS

Servings: 4 tortillas | Prep Time: 10 minutes | Cooking Time: 5 minutes

Ingredients:

- 1 cup (110 g) almond flour
- 1 Tbsp. coconut flour
- 1 Tbsp. xanthan gum
- 1 whole egg, beaten
- 3 Tbsp. water
- ¼ tsp. kosher salt
- ½ tsp. low carb baking powder

Steps:

1. Transfer all of the ingredients into a food processor and pulse in five-second intervals until fully combined and smooth.
2. Take the formed dough out of the food processor and wrap it tightly in cling film. Let the dough rest at room temperature for about 15 minutes.
3. Next, unwrap the dough and divide it into four separate chunks. Roll the chunks into a ball and place them between two sheets of parchment paper.
4. With a rolling pin, roll the dough until you get a very thin round disc. Meanwhile, heat a non-stick skillet over medium-high heat.
5. Carefully peel your formed disks from the parchment paper and transfer them onto the hot skillet and cook until slightly charred on both sides.
6. Serve while still warm, or cool completely and store in a Ziploc bag for up to three days.

<u>Baking Tip</u>

- Be very careful when peeling the tortilla off the parchment paper as it is prone to ripping.

Nutritional Facts (Per Serving):

Calories 198, Fat 13 g, Carbohydrates 9 g, Protein 8 g

GREEN TORTILLAS

Servings: 1 tortilla | Prep Time: 5 minutes | Cooking Time: 5 minutes

Ingredients:

- 2 Tbsp. flaxseed meal
- 1 whole egg
- ¼ cup (60 g) spinach
- ¼ tsp. garlic powder
- ¼ tsp. low carb baking powder
- 1 Tbsp. water

Steps:

1. Grease an eight-inch glass pie dish with cooking spray or coconut oil and set aside.
2. In a food processor, combine egg, spinach, water, flaxseed, garlic powder, and baking powder. Process until smooth and thoroughly combined.
3. Transfer the mixture into the prepared pie dish, making sure that it is uniform and smooth.
4. Place the dish in the microwave and microwave on high for 3-4 minutes.
5. Remove, and let it stand for 1 or 2 minutes.
6. Gently remove the tortilla from the pan and let cool slightly until easy enough to handle. Serve immediately.

Baking Tip

- Scrambled egg and avocado go amazingly well with this quick tortilla.

Nutritional Facts (Per Serving):

Calories 151, Fat 9.4 g, Carbohydrates 5.8 g, Protein 9.2 g

ASSORTED BUNS & BAGELS

Cheese Buns

Sandwich Bagels

Seeded Bagels

Vegetable Bagels

Cheese Bagels

CHEESE BUNS

Servings: 4 buns | Prep Time: 10 minutes | Cooking Time: 13 minutes

Ingredients:

- 1¼ cups (140 g) almond flour
- 2 oz. (60 g) cream cheese
- 2 Tbsp. oat fiber
- 1½ cups (170 g) shredded mozzarella
- 1 large egg
- 1 Tbsp. low carb baking powder

Steps:

1. Line a baking sheet with parchment paper and preheat your oven to 400°F (205°C).
2. Let the mozzarella and cream cheese melt in a microwave for around one minute. Using a food processor, mix the two together along with an egg. Blend until smooth and emulsified.
3. Add the flour, oat fiber, and baking powder to the food processor mixture and process until a sticky dough is formed. If you find the dough too sticky, allow it to stand for a few minutes until cooler and try again.
4. Oil your hands with olive oil slightly, shape your dough into four buns, and arrange them on your baking sheet two inches apart.
5. Bake for around 13 minutes and allow the buns to cool on the baking sheet before cutting and serving.
6. Store these buns for up to 10 days in your refrigerator or freeze them for up to four months.

Baking Tip:

- Sprinkle your buns with sesame seeds before placing them in the oven!

Nutritional Facts (Per Serving):

Calories 250, Fat 25 g, Carbohydrates 7 g, Protein 14 g

SANDWICH BAGELS

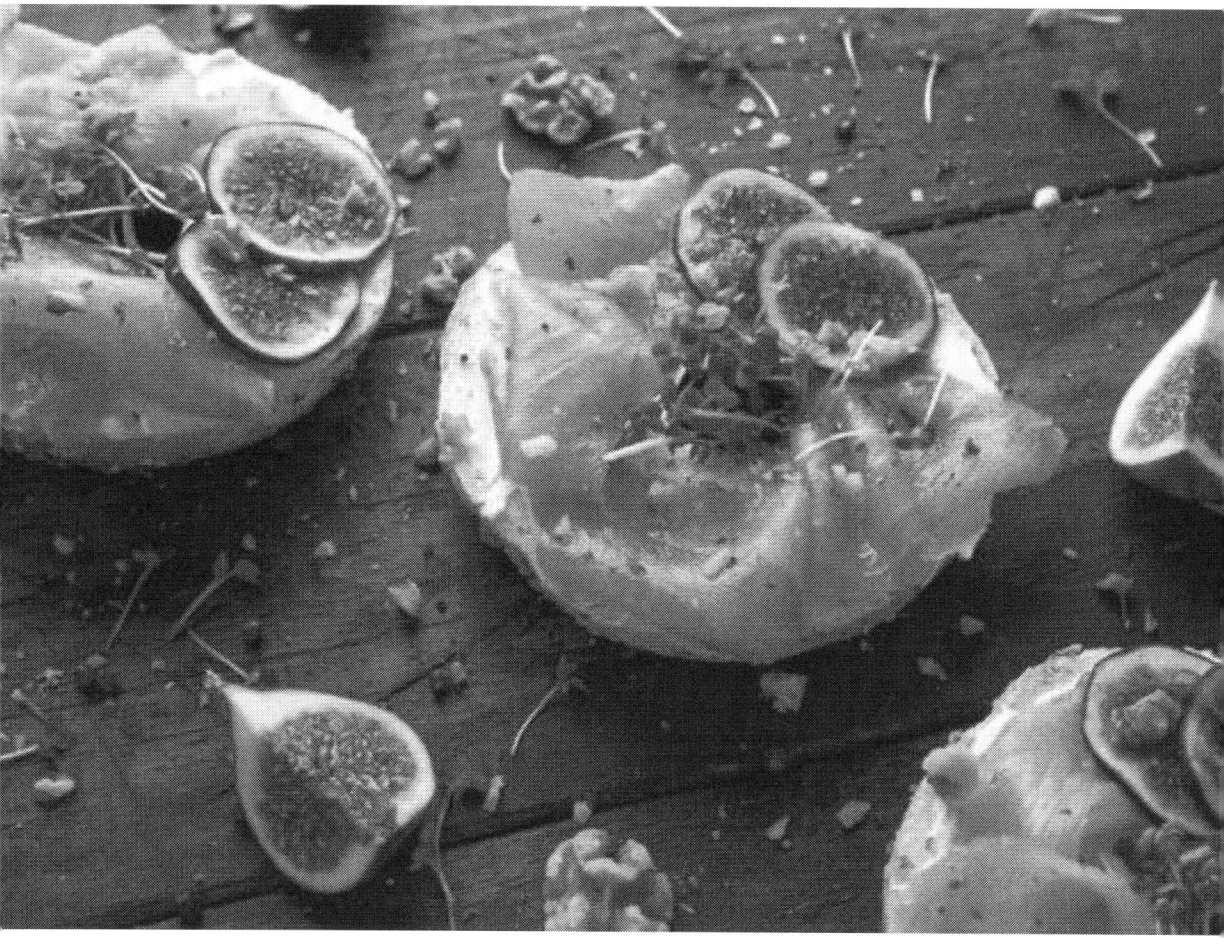

Servings: 6 bagels | Prep Time: 10 minutes | Cooking Time: 30 minutes

Ingredients:

- ¾ cup (85 g) almond flour
- ¼ cup (30 g) coconut flour
- ¼ cup (40 g) ground flaxseed
- 3 Tbsp. psyllium husk powder
- 1 cup (240 ml) boiling water
- 3 egg whites
- 2½ Tbsp. apple cider vinegar
- ½ cup (30 g) sun-dried tomatoes, chopped
- 1 tsp. rosemary
- 1 tsp. garlic, minced
- ½ tsp. kosher salt
- 2 tsp. low carb baking powder

Steps:

1. Preheat your oven to 350°F (180°C) and grease a donut pan. Set aside.
2. Mix psyllium husk powder, coconut flour, almond flour, salt, flaxseed, baking powder, and oregano.
3. Add sun-dried tomatoes, garlic, vinegar, egg whites, and boiling water. Mix until a thick dough forms.
4. Divide the dough into six portions and place it in the donut pan.
5. Bake for 30 minutes until the bagels are firm to touch.
6. Let the bagels cool completely before taking them out of the pan and serving.
7. The product can be stored in an air-tight container in the refrigerator for up to five days or frozen for up to three months.

Baking Tip

- Perfect with plain cream cheese and salmon fillet slices.

Nutritional Facts (Per Serving):

Calories 120, Fat 4.7 g, Carbohydrates 11.8 g, Protein 9.4 g

SEEDED BAGELS

Servings: 6 bagels | Prep Time: 15 minutes | Cooking Time: 38 minutes

Ingredients:

- ½ cup +1 Tbsp. (70 g) coconut flour
- ¾ cup (180 ml) coconut milk
- 3 Tbsp. coconut oil
- 3 whole eggs
- 1 egg white
- 2 Tbsp. sesame seeds/poppy seeds
- 1 Tbsp. gelatin
- ¼ tsp. kosher salt
- ¼ tsp. low carb baking powder

Steps:

1. Grease a donut pan and preheat the oven to 350°F (180°C). Set aside.
2. Mix coconut oil, coconut flour, eggs, gelatin, coconut milk, salt, and baking powder until homogeneous and a smooth batter forms.
3. Pour this batter into the donut molds.
4. Brush your batter with egg whites and sprinkle with sesame seeds.
5. Place in your oven and bake for 30 - 38 minutes. Your bagels should be firm to the touch once done.
6. Allow your bagels to cool fully in the molds before removing and serving.

Baking Tip

- For an extra coconut element, sprinkle additionally with desiccated coconut.

Nutritional Facts (Per Serving):

Calories 153, Fat 11.5 g, Carbohydrates 6.8 g, Protein 6.4 g

VEGETABLE BAGELS

Servings: 4 bagels | Prep Time: 15 minutes | Cooking Time: 22 minutes

Ingredients:

- ¼ cup (30 g) coconut flour
- ¼ cup (30 g) almond flour
- 4 cups (400 g) cauliflower, finely chopped and cooked
- 2 cups (230 g) shredded mozzarella cheese
- 4 whole eggs
- 2 tsp. low carb baking powder

Steps:

1. Line a baking sheet with parchment paper and heat the oven to 400°F (205°C).
2. Dry your cooked and chopped cauliflower until there is little to no moisture. Either do this by microwaving it and stirring at 15-second intervals or with a kitchen towel.
3. Add your cauliflower, three eggs (the last egg is saved for the egg wash), flours, baking powder, and mozzarella, and mix until combined and a cohesive batter is formed.
4. Carefully spoon the batter into a half measuring cup and press it down so that it does not crumble during the next step.
5. Quickly (like building sandcastles!), turn the cup over onto the baking sheet. If you press down the batter enough, it should hold its shape after the cup is removed. To shape the bagels, simply use your finger to create a hole in the middle. Do your best to make sure that the surface of your bagel is smooth and even.
6. Whisk the remaining egg and brush over the top of your bagels.
7. Place your bagels in the oven and bake for 28 minutes. You will know they are done when they are golden brown and spring back when pressed down on.
8. You can keep these bagels in the fridge for up to four days.

<u>Baking Tip</u>

- Try to get your cauliflower as dry as possible, so the bagels hold together when baked.

Nutritional Facts (Per Serving):

Calories 230, Fat 13.2 g, Carbohydrates 11 g, Protein 17.5 g

CHEESE BAGELS

Servings: 7 bagels | Prep Time: 10 minutes | Cooking Time: 12 minutes

Ingredients:

- 1¾ cups (200 g) almond flour
- 2 large eggs, beaten
- 1½ cups (170 g) shredded mozzarella
- 1 cup (90 g) shredded parmesan
- 2 oz. (60 g) cream cheese
- 1 tsp. minced garlic
- 1 tsp. oregano
- ½ tsp. basil
- ¼ tsp. kosher salt
- 1 Tbsp. low carb baking powder

Steps:

1. Set aside a baking sheet lined with parchment paper and preheat the oven to 400°F (205°C).
2. Mix parmesan, mozzarella, and cream cheese together in a bowl before melting it in the microwave.
3. In another bowl, mix together eggs, flour, garlic, and the melted cheese. Use your hands or the paddle attachment if using a stand mixer. This dough will be quite sticky, so it is recommended to oil your hands a little if you're handling it.
4. Divide the dough into seven parts and roll out each one into a long tube shape. Bring the ends together to create a bagel shape, and place it on your prepared baking sheet.
5. Once all of your bagels are nicely smooth and well-formed, sprinkle the tops with salt and place them in the oven. Bake for 12 minutes until lightly golden.
6. Allow to cool for 20 minutes on the baking sheet before transferring them onto a cooling rack to cool completely.
7. If you'd like to store these bagels for longer than a week, you can freeze them for up to four months.

<u>Baking Tip</u>

- Oiling your hands will ensure that the dough doesn't stick to them.

Nutritional Facts (Per Serving):

Calories 210, Fat 15 g, Carbohydrates 6 g, Protein 14 g

SNACK BREADSTICKS & CRACKERS

Cheese Breadsticks

Mozzarella Breadsticks

Sesame Seed Breadsticks

Sunflower Seed Breadsticks

Keto Breadsticks

Spicy Crackers

CHEESE BREADSTICKS

Servings: 6 breadsticks | Prep Time: 10 minutes | Cooking Time: 20 minutes

Ingredients:

- ⅔ cup (85 g) coconut flour
- 3 cups (340 g) shredded mozzarella cheese
- 4 whole eggs
- 4 Tbsp. cream cheese
- 1 Tbsp. butter, melted
- 1 tsp. garlic powder
- 1 tsp. Italian herbs
- 1 tsp. kosher salt
- 1 tsp. low carb baking powder
- 1 Tbsp. pumpkin seeds, for sprinkling
- 1 cup water as needed

Steps:

1. Line a baking sheet with parchment paper and heat your oven to 350°F (180°C).
2. Melt the shredded mozzarella cheese with the cream cheese in the microwave. Stir to make sure they are well combined.
3. Add garlic powder, eggs, flour, oregano, and salt. Mix again to form a ball of dough. If your dough is too hard and it is not coming together, add water one Tbsp. at a time until the dough sticks together.
4. Using oiled hands, divide the dough into eight portions and shape it into your perfect breadstick shape on your baking sheet.
5. Brush your breadsticks with melted butter and place in the oven for 20 minutes. Your breadsticks should be firm to touch and lightly golden brown at the end of baking.
6. Breadsticks can be stored in an air-tight container for up to three days.

Baking Tip

- Experiment with the types of herbs you use in this batter.

Nutritional Facts (Per Serving):

Calories 248, Fat 14 g, Carbohydrates 4 g, Protein 17 g

MOZZARELLA BREADSTICKS

Servings: 6 breadsticks | Prep Time: 10 minutes | Cooking Time: 15 minutes

Ingredients:

- ⅓ cup (45 g) coconut flour
- 3½ cups (400 g) shredded mozzarella
- 1½ cups (140 g) parmesan, grated
- 4½ Tbsp. unsalted butter, melted and cooled
- 1 oz. (30 g) cream cheese
- 4 whole eggs
- 1 tsp. oregano
- ½ tsp. garlic powder
- ¼ tsp. kosher salt
- ¼ tsp. low carb baking powder

Steps:

1. Set the oven to 400°F (205°C) and line a baking sheet with parchment paper. Set aside.
2. Mix together cream cheese, melted butter, salt, and eggs in a large bowl until well combined.
3. Add flour, oregano, garlic powder, ½ cup parmesan, and 1½ cups mozzarella. Mix until thoroughly combined. A thick batter should be formed.
4. Transfer the batter onto the baking sheet and sprinkle the top with the remainder of the cheese.
5. Place in the oven for 15 minutes until lightly golden and firm to touch.
6. Allow to cool before cutting into individual breadsticks and serve while warm.

<u>Baking Tip:</u>

- This batter is quite sticky, so be careful when handling it!

Nutritional Facts (Per Serving):

Calories 299, Fat 17 g, Carbohydrates 4 g, Protein 23 g

SESAME SEED BREADSTICKS

Servings: 4 breadsticks | Prep Time: 10 minutes | Cooking Time: 15 minutes

Ingredients:

- ¾ cup (85 g) almond flour
- 1½ cups (170 g) shredded mozzarella cheese
- 2 Tbsp. cream cheese
- 3 Tbsp. butter, melted
- 1 Tbsp. sesame seeds
- ¼ tsp. kosher salt

Steps:

1. Preheat your oven to 400°F (205°C) and put parchment paper on your baking sheet.
2. Melt grated mozzarella along with cream cheese in the microwave and mix until homogeneous.
3. Combine with flour and salt until smooth. If you feel that the dough is becoming too sticky, add 1 tablespoon of almond flour until it is easier to handle.
4. Place the dough on parchment paper, and with a rolling pin, roll the dough out until it is ½ inch thick. Cut the rolled-out dough into long breadsticks and place these breadsticks onto the prepared baking sheet.
5. Brush your breadsticks with melted butter and sprinkle generously with sesame seeds.
6. Place in the oven for 15 minutes. Your breadsticks should be golden brown at the end of baking.
7. Allow to cool completely before serving. Alternatively, you can freeze it for up to four months.

<u>Baking Tip</u>

- Feel free to sprinkle the "Everything Bagel" seasoning on this breadstick.

Nutritional Facts (Per Serving):

Calories 90, Fat 11 g, Carbohydrates 1 g, Protein 5 g

SUNFLOWER SEED BREADSTICKS

Servings: 6 breadsticks | Prep Time: 10 minutes | Cooking Time: 12 minutes

Ingredients:

- ¾ cup (90 g) shredded mozzarella
- ⅔ cup (90 g) sunflower seeds
- 4 Tbsp. cream cheese
- 1 whole egg
- 2 tsp. psyllium husk powder
- 2 tsp. rosemary
- ½ tsp. coarse kosher salt
- sesame seeds for sprinkling (optional)
- ½ tsp. fine kosher salt

Steps:

1. Preheat your oven to 400°F (205°C) and prepare a parchment-lined baking sheet.
2. Place the sunflower seeds in a food processor and process them on high until the sunflower seeds form a flour.
3. Place this flour in a bowl along with 1 tsp. of rosemary, salt, and psyllium husks. Whisk until fully combined, and set aside.
4. Melt cream cheese and mozzarella together in a microwave. Allow a few minutes to cool and add to the dry ingredient mix.
5. With slightly oiled hands, form breadstick shapes from the dough and place each one on the baking sheet.
6. Score the breadsticks a couple of times with a sharp knife. Sprinkle with the rest of the rosemary and sesame seeds, and place in the oven for 22 minutes or until beautifully golden.
7. Once out of the oven, sprinkle with coarse kosher salt.
8. Allow to cool before serving. You can keep the food in an air-tight container for up to four days.

Baking Tips

- Sprinkle the kosher salt after your breadsticks have cooled a little, so it remains on the surface but still sticks.

Nutritional Facts (Per Serving):

Calories 55, Fat 4 g, Carbohydrates 1 g, Protein 2 g

KETO BREADSTICKS

Servings: 4 breadsticks | Prep Time: 10 minutes | Cooking Time: 32 minutes

Ingredients:

- 2 cups (230 g) riced cauliflower
- 1 cup (110 g) shredded mozzarella
- ¼ cup (20 g) parmesan cheese
- 2 whole eggs
- ½ tsp. garlic powder
- 1 tsp. Italian seasoning
- ½ tsp. black pepper
- ½ tsp. kosher salt

Steps:

1. Line a baking sheet with parchment paper and preheat your oven to 350°F (180°C).
2. Place eggs, cauliflower, garlic, cheese, pepper, Italian seasoning, and salt in a food processor. Process until homogeneous, and the cauliflower is well broken down.
3. Transfer the mixture onto your prepared baking sheet, and smooth out.
4. Bake for 30 minutes until lightly golden.
5. Take your batter out of the oven and sprinkle it with parmesan cheese.
6. Turn on the broiler and put the batter underneath for about 2–3 minutes or until the cheese has melted and begins bubbling.
7. Allow to cool completely before cutting. Serve when warm.

<u>Baking Tips</u>

- These breadsticks are perfect on their own as a snack.

Nutritional Facts (Per Serving):

Calories 165, Fat 14 g, Carbohydrates 5 g, Protein 17 g

SPICY CRACKERS

Servings: 30 crackers | Prep Time: 12 minutes | Cooking Time: 10 minutes

Ingredients:

- ¾ cup (85 g) almond flour
- 1 cup (110 g) shredded mozzarella cheese
- 1 cup (90 g) cheddar cheese, grated
- 2 Tbsp. cream cheese
- 1 whole egg
- Cajun seasoning to taste

Steps:

1. Set your oven to 400°F (205°C) and line a baking tray with parchment paper.
2. In a bowl, combine mozzarella, cheddar, and cream cheese. Place in a microwave and melt until you can stir the cheese to make a smooth ball.
3. Add almond flour to the cheese and stir to combine. If the mixture is too stiff, heat up in the microwave for 30 more seconds.
4. Once the mixture is homogeneous, add Cajun seasoning to taste.
5. Mix in the egg until fully incorporated and a smooth dough is formed.
6. Transfer this dough onto a sheet of parchment paper and cover it with another. With a rolling pin, roll out the dough. You are in control of how thick or how thin you would like your crackers to be.
7. Cut your dough into squares. Transfer your cut squares onto your prepared baking sheet.
8. Place in the oven for 10 minutes. Your baked crackers should be golden brown in color.
9. Allow to cool fully before serving, or refrigerate for up to four days.

<u>Baking Tips</u>

- This recipe can make you a dozen crackers without much effort. Simply double or triple the ingredients!

Nutritional Facts (Per Serving):

Calories 238, Fat 19 g, Carbohydrates 3 g, Protein 13 g

DELICATE MUFFINS & SCONES

Traditional Pumpkin Scones

Savory Bacon Scones

Egg Muffins

Berry Muffins

Citrus Muffins

Cocoa Muffins

TRADITIONAL PUMPKIN SCONES

Servings: 8 scones | Prep Time: 10 minutes | Cooking Time: 20 minutes

- 2½ cups (280 g) almond flour
- ⅓ cup (40 g) coconut flour
- 1 cup (225 g) pumpkin puree
- ⅓ cup (70 g) erythritol
- ¼ cup (60 g) unsalted butter
- 2 whole eggs
- 1 egg white
- 1 Tbsp. heavy cream
- 1 Tbsp. sugar-free pumpkin syrup
- 1 Tbsp. bourbon
- 1½ tsp. cinnamon
- 1 tsp. ginger
- ¼ tsp. nutmeg
- ½ tsp. cloves
- Handful pumpkin seeds
- ¼ tsp. kosher salt
- 1 tsp. low carb baking powder

Steps:

1. Line your baking sheet with parchment paper and preheat the oven to 325°F (160°C).
2. Place the pumpkin puree on a piece of paper with a kitchen towel. Place another kitchen towel on top of your pumpkin and press until the pumpkin is as dry as you can get it. Set aside.
3. Place the butter in a small saucepan and melt over medium to low heat, continuously stirring. Wait until the butter appears golden brown in color, but watch it carefully as it is prone to burning and turning too dark.
4. Once this is complete, take it off the heat and cool down for a few minutes.
5. In a large bowl, mix flour, salt, baking powder, spices, and sweetener together. Whisk until homogeneous.
6. Mix together eggs, bourbon, pumpkin syrup, heavy cream, and pumpkin puree in a separate bowl. Mix until well combined and smooth. Add this to your previously mixed dry ingredients.
7. Next, add the melted butter and mix until a firm dough forms.
8. Transfer this dough to your baking sheet and form it into a large circle shape. Cut the circle into 12 slices.
9. Brush the top of the dough with egg whites and sprinkle with pumpkin seeds.
10. Place in the oven and bake for 30 minutes, until lightly golden and firm to touch.
11. Cool completely before serving. You can store them for up to 5 days in air-tight containers.

Baking Tip

- You can whip some cream cheese and put it on top of your muffin for extra flavor.

Nutritional Facts (Per Serving):

Calories 214, Fat 17 g, Carbohydrates 9 g, Protein 7 g

SAVORY BACON SCONES

Servings: 6 scones | Prep Time: 15 minutes | Cooking Time: 10 minutes

Ingredients:

- 1½ cups (170 g) almond flour
- ¼ cup (30 g) coconut flour
- ¼ cup (40 g) ground flaxseeds
- ½ cup (55 g) cheddar cheese, grated
- 3 Tbsp. unsweetened almond milk
- 4 slices (60 g) of bacon
- 3 Tbsp. chopped chives
- 2 whole eggs
- ¼ tsp. black pepper
- ¼ tsp. kosher salt
- 1 tsp. low carb baking powder

Steps:

1. Line a baking sheet with parchment paper and preheat your oven to 350°F (180°C).
2. Prepare a big bowl and mix flours, ground flaxseeds, baking powder, chives, cheese, salt, and pepper. Set aside.
3. Cut your bacon finely, and fry in a non-stick pan for about four minutes until cooked. Allow some time to cool.
4. In a small bowl, combine eggs and almond milk, and beat with a fork until combined. Add this to the dry ingredients. Fold to form the dough.
5. Next, add the cooked bacon and fold once more to incorporate.
6. Transfer the dough onto a square of parchment paper. Cover with another square before rolling the dough out.
7. Cut the dough with a 2½-inch cookie cutter, and place it on your prepared baking sheet.
8. Cook for 15 minutes in the oven, until golden brown and firm to touch.
9. Allow to cool completely before serving.
10. Refrigerate for up to one week.

<u>Baking Tip</u>

- Sprinkle the scones with cheese before placing them in the oven for an extra cheesy punch.

Nutritional Facts (Per Serving):

Calories 129, Fat 10.6 g, Carbohydrates 1.4 g, Protein 5.7 g

EGG MUFFINS

Servings: 10 muffins | Prep Time: 10 minutes | Cooking Time: 25 minutes

Ingredients:

- 1 cup (110 g) almond flour
- ¼ cup (30 g) coconut flour
- 1 cup (110 g) shredded cheddar cheese
- 4 oz. (120 g) finely diced jalapenos
- 4 whole eggs
- ½ cup (120 g) unsalted butter, softened
- ½ cup (120 ml) sour cream
- 2 Tbsp. sweetener of your choice
- ½ tsp. kosher salt
- 1 Tbsp. low carb baking powder

Steps:

1. With an electric mixer, cream together butter and sweetener until the butter is lighter in color, combined with the sweetener, and appears fluffy.
2. One at a time, add eggs until completely incorporated before adding sour cream. Beat until smooth.
3. Add baking powder, flour, and salt, and beat again until combined.
4. Softly fold in the jalapenos and cheddar cheese until well spread out throughout the batter.
5. Once combined, pour the batter into the muffin tin. Optionally, sprinkle some cheddar cheese on top.
6. Place into the oven and bake for 25 minutes at 350°F (180°C), or until an inserted toothpick comes out clean.
7. Allow to cool fully in the muffin tin before removing and serving.
8. Store in an air-tight container in the refrigerator for up to five days.

<u>Baking Tip</u>

- Adjust the spice by varying the quantity of jalapenos.

Nutritional Facts (Per Serving):

Calories 206, Fat 18 g, Carbohydrates 3.5 g, Protein 6 g

BERRY MUFFINS

Servings: 6 muffins | Prep Time: 10 minutes | Cooking Time: 30 minutes

Ingredients:

- 2½ cups (280 g) almond flour
- ½ cup (90 g) fresh blueberries
- 3 whole eggs
- 5 oz. (140 g) full-fat Greek yogurt
- ½ tsp. vanilla extract
- ½ cup granulated sweetener of your choice
- ¼ tsp. kosher salt
- 2 tsp. low carb baking powder
- A cup of water to add as needed

Steps:

1. Preheat your oven to 325°F (160°C) and line a muffin tray with muffin liners.
2. In a blender, mix together eggs, yogurt, vanilla, and salt.
3. Add the sweetener, flour, and baking powder and continue blending until a smooth batter forms without lumps. If you find that your batter is too thick, add water one tablespoon at a time. Your batter should be the texture of thick pancake batter.
4. Slowly stir in your blueberries before pouring your batter into your muffin liners. Bake these for 25–30 minutes until an inserted toothpick comes out clean.
5. You can freeze these muffins for three months or store them in an air-tight container for up to five days.

<u>Baking Tip</u>

- The yogurt in this recipe ensures that the muffins are extremely moist.

Nutritional Facts (Per Serving):

Calories 163, Fat 12.9 g, Carbohydrates 6.5 g, Protein 7.7 g

CITRUS MUFFINS

Servings: 10 muffins | Prep Time: 10 minutes | Cooking Time: 25 minutes

Ingredients:

- 2½ cups (280 g) almond flour
- ⅓ cup (80 ml) unsweetened almond milk
- ½ cup granulated sweetener of your choice
- 2 large eggs
- ⅓ cup (80 ml) avocado oil
- 1 Tbsp. poppy seeds
- 1 Tbsp. ground flaxseeds
- Zest and juice of one lemon
- 2 tsp. low carb baking powder

Steps:

1. Preheat oven to 350°F (180°C) and line a muffin tray with muffin liners. Set aside.
2. Whisk together poppy seeds, flaxseeds, baking powder, sweetener, and flour.
3. Next, add the almond milk, eggs, avocado oil, lemon zest and juice, and eggs. Mix until completely homogenous and smooth.
4. Pour the batter into your prepared muffin tray and place in the oven.
5. Bake for 20–25 minutes or until an inserted toothpick comes out clean. The muffins should be lightly golden in color at the end of baking.
6. Store in an air-tight container for up to three days, or freeze for one month.

Nutritional Facts (Per Serving):

Calories 268, Fat 24 g, Carbohydrates 3 g, Protein 8 g

COCOA MUFFINS

Servings: 10 muffins | Prep Time: 10 minutes | Cooking Time: 20 minutes

Ingredients:

- 2 cups (225 g) almond flour
- ⅓ cup (80 ml) unsweetened almond milk
- 3 whole eggs, beaten
- ½ cup (120 g) unsalted butter, melted and cooled
- ½ cup (100 g) Monk fruit sweetener
- ¾ cup (75 g) unsweetened cocoa powder
- ¾ cup (170 g) unsweetened chocolate chips
- 1 tsp. vanilla extract
- ¼ tsp. kosher salt
- 2 tsp. low carb baking powder

Steps:

1. Preheat your oven to 350°F (180°C) and put muffin liners in muffin cups.
2. Mix together almond flour, salt, baking powder, cocoa powder, and sweetener in a large bowl.
3. Add eggs, almond milk, butter, and vanilla extract. Mix again until a smooth batter is formed.
4. Fold in the chocolate chips until well spread out in the batter.
5. Pour the batter into the prepared muffin liners and place in the oven.
6. Bake for about 20 minutes or until an inserted toothpick comes out clean.
7. Allow to cool completely before serving. Keep in an air-tight container for up to 1 week, or freeze for up to 3 months.

Baking Tip

- You can always add white chocolate chips to your batter.

Nutritional Facts (Per Serving):

Calories 206, Fat 19 g, Carbohydrates 2 g, Protein 7 g

MOUTHWATERING WAFFLES & PANCAKES

Pancakes with Raspberries

Pancakes with Chocolate Chips

Belgian WaffleS

Cocoa Waffles

Sweet Crepes

PANCAKES WITH RASPBERRIES

Servings: 8 pancakes | Prep Time: 10 minutes | Cooking Time: 30 minutes

Ingredients:

- 1½ cup (170 g) almond flour
- ¼ cup (60 ml) full almond milk
- 2 whole eggs
- 1 Tbsp. tapioca flour
- ¼ cup (60 ml) sugar-free maple syrup
- 2 Tbsp. vanilla extract
- ¼ tsp. kosher salt
- ½ tsp. baking soda

Steps:

1. Preheat a non-stick pan on medium heat.
2. Mix together salt, almond flour, tapioca flour, and baking soda in a medium bowl.
3. Once homogenous, add eggs, milk, vanilla extract, and maple syrup. Mix until well combined and the smooth batter has formed.
4. Using a ¼ measuring cup, spoon the mixture onto your preheated frying pan.
5. Cook until the edges start browning and the top starts burning before flipping over and cooking for an additional 2-3 minutes.
6. Serve while still hot.

Baking Tip

- Feel free to add raspberries or unsweetened chocolate chips to these delicious pancakes.

Nutritional Facts (Per Serving):

Calories 148, Fat 7.5 g, Carbohydrates 8.6 g, Protein 8 g

PANCAKES WITH CHOCOLATE CHIPS

Servings: 5 pancakes | Prep Time: 5 minutes | Cooking Time: 10 minutes

Ingredients:

- 1 cup (110 g) almond flour
- ½ cup (120 ml) almond milk
- 2 whole eggs
- 1 Tbsp. salted butter, melted
- 1½ tsp. banana extract
- 1/3 cup (70 g) Swerve sweetener
- ¼ tsp. cinnamon
- ¼ tsp. kosher salt
- 1 tsp. low carb baking powder

Steps:

1. Preheat a non-stick pan on medium-high heat.
2. Whisk eggs, butter, and almond milk in a food processor.
3. Add banana extract, sweetener, flour, baking powder, salt, and cinnamon.
4. Process until fully combined and a smooth batter forms.
5. Using a ¼ measuring cup, spoon the batter gently onto the preheated pan.
6. Cook until the edges begin to brown and the top starts to gently bubble.
7. Flip over and cook for an additional minute before serving and topping with your favorite toppings.

Baking Tip

- Adding chocolate chips to your pancakes will give them an extra "something special."

Nutritional Facts (Per Serving):

Calories 256, Fat 22.5 g, Carbohydrates 5.6 g, Protein 8 g

BELGIAN WAFFLES

Servings: 8 waffles | Prep Time: 15 minutes | Cooking Time: 30 minutes

Ingredients:
- ⅔ cup (75 g) almond flour
- ¼ cup (30 g) coconut flour
- 1 cup (240 ml) water
- 3 whole eggs, beaten
- ¼ cup (60 g) unsalted butter, softened
- 1 tsp. xanthan gum
- 1 Tbsp. psyllium husk powder
- 3 Tbsp. sweetener of your choice
- 1 tsp. vanilla extract
- ¼ tsp. kosher salt
- 1½ tsp. low carb baking powder

Steps:
1. In a medium bowl, combine together flour, xanthan gum, and psyllium husk powder. Set aside.
2. In a medium pot, heat up water, butter, and sweetener until it begins to simmer. Gradually add the flour mixture while continuously stirring. Continue to heat until firm dough forms that come apart from the pot's sides.
3. Transfer the dough into a bowl and allow a few minutes to cool.
4. After the dough has cooled significantly, add eggs to the dough and mix with an electric mixer. When the eggs are fully incorporated, add baking powder and vanilla extract.
5. Allow the dough to rest for around 10 minutes.
6. While the dough is resting, preheat your waffle maker. Make sure to grease it very well.
7. Spoon the batter into your waffle maker and gently close. Cook your waffles for no longer than 12 minutes at a time.
8. Store in an air-tight container at room temperature for up to three days.

<u>Baking Tips</u>
- Top with your favorite ice cream or fruit for a delicious dessert.

Nutritional Facts (Per Serving):
Calories 140, Fat 11 g, Carbohydrates 4 g, Protein 4 g

COCOA WAFFLES

Servings: 5 waffles | Prep Time: 15 minutes | Cooking Time: 20 minutes

Ingredients:

- 4 Tbsp. coconut flour
- 1 stick (110 g) butter, melted
- 4 large eggs, separated
- 3 Tbsp. full-fat milk
- 4 Tbsp. sweetener of your choice
- ¼ cup (25 g) unsweetened cocoa powder
- 2 tsp. vanilla extract
- 1 tsp. low carb baking powder

Steps:

1. In a medium bowl, beat egg whites until light, fluffy and stiff peaks form when the whisk is lifted. Set aside.
2. Mix together egg yolks, sweetener, cocoa powder, flour, and baking powder in a separate bowl.
3. Once that is incorporated, add butter, milk, and vanilla extract. Mix until homogeneous.
4. Grease and preheat your waffle maker.
5. Next, very gently fold the beaten egg whites into your mixture until fully combined. The batter should look fluffy and smooth.
6. Spoon the batter into your preheated waffle maker and close. Cook for about 18 minutes.
7. For up to three days, store in air tight containers.

<u>Baking Tip</u>

- I suggest serving with whipped cream, strawberries, and chocolate syrup for a Black Forest taste.

Nutritional Facts (Per Serving):

Calories 289, Fat 26 g, Carbohydrates 7.6 g, Protein 7.2 g

SWEET CREPES

Servings: 4 crepes | Prep Time: 10 minutes | Cooking Time: 10 minutes

Ingredients:

- ¼ cup (30 g) almond flour
- 4 whole eggs
- 1 tsp. vanilla extract
- 1 Tbsp. coconut oil
- ¼ tsp. ground cinnamon
- 1 Tbsp. sweetener of your choice

Steps:

1. On medium to low heat, preheat a non-stick frying pan.
2. In a large bowl, combine almond flour, eggs, vanilla, cinnamon, and sweetener. Whisk until fully combined and a smooth batter forms.
3. Grease the preheated pan with coconut oil.
4. Spoon your batter into the pan using a ¼ measuring cup. Tilt the pan to spread the batter all around the bottom of your pan.
5. Set down and let cook until the sides of the crepe start to crisp up.
6. Using a rubber spatula, loosen the pancake from the pan, and with one fluid motion, flip the pancake over. Cook the pancake for a further minute or two before transferring to a plate and serving while still warm.

Baking Tip

- Serve these crepes with coconut whipped cream and melted unsweetened chocolate.

Nutritional Facts (Per Serving):

Calories 127, Fat 8.5 g, Carbohydrates 4.6 g, Protein 7.6 g

From the Author

I've been a **professional chef for over fifteen years** and a passionate advocate for the **ketogenic diet.** My areas of expertise include **recipe development, healthy meal plans, and professional cooking.** I help people to be healthier while still enjoying delicious food.

I have loved baking since my childhood. I always collect new recipes as well as develop my own. First, I learned how to bake classic pies and then plunged into traditional European recipes. Next, I studied the art of baking with the best American and European chefs.

Most of all, I like to experiment with bread. **Variations of baking with different kinds of flour opened incredible opportunities for creativity. As a result,** I've developed and baked bread for both ketogenic and Paleo diets. It's gluten-free and grain-free as well.

Delicious bread exists for any occasion, and it decorates any table from everyday to festive. So my friends always know that they can eat my fresh, fragrant bread.

I'm baking at work and home. In the bakery, my assistants help me, and the technologists and cooks improve the recipes and methods of baking. At home, I bake with my family, and even the children participate in this fascinating process.

And I generously share my keto bread recipes and the secrets of mastery with my readers. So let your house be filled with the cozy smell of freshly baked bread!

Our Recommendations

Keto Bread Machine Cookbook: Easy Keto Bread Recipes for Effortless Baking in Your Bread Maker

*If you enjoy the book or find it useful, leave your **review** of the book, please. Your feedback is essential for other readers and us to make the right choice.*

Copyright

ALL ©COPYRIGHTS RESERVED 2018 by Jennifer Tate

All Rights Reserved. No part of this publication or the information in it may be quoted from or reproduced in any form by means such as printing, scanning, photocopying, or otherwise without prior written permission of the copyright holder.

Disclaimer and Terms of Use: Effort has been made to ensure that the information in this book is accurate and complete; however, the author and the publisher do not warrant the accuracy of the information, text, or graphics contained within the book due to the rapidly changing nature of science, research, known and unknown facts, and the internet. The author and the publisher do not hold any responsibility for errors, omissions, or contrary interpretation of the subject matter herein. This book is presented solely for motivational and informational purposes only

Printed in Great Britain
by Amazon